The heart-traveller

1

Sri Chinmoy

Aspiration-Flames
Aspiration and God's Hour

Ganapati Press

© 2019 SRI CHINMOY CENTRE

ISBN 978-1-911319-24-5

Cover drawing: *Soul-Bird* by Sri Chinmoy. Blue pen on ruled paper, 5 January 2005. Lambert collection, Lyon, France.

FIRST EDITION WENT TO PRESS ON 16 JUNE 2019

Aspiration-Flames

Aspiration-Flames

How do we aspire?

Sri Chinmoy: Cry, cry like a child from the very depths of your heart. There is no prayer that cannot be answered, no meditation that cannot be fulfilled if you cry sincerely. Aspiration is your soul's mounting cry to reach the Highest and to bring down the Highest into the earth's consciousness.

What is aspiration?

Sri Chinmoy: Aspiration is inner cry. Aspiration is inner courage. What is inner courage? Inner courage is implicit faith in your own divine Pilot. If you have inner courage, that means you have faith in your Master.

How can we recognise true aspiration?

Sri Chinmoy: This question is most interesting and at the same time most instructive. Sometimes an aspirant feels that he is doing the right thing. He feels that he is doing his best in his aspiration and that God is most pleased with him. But it may be that this person's aspiration is absolutely insincere. His aspiration may be next to nothing at that very time.

Now, how can we know whether our aspiration is genuine, sincere and productive? There is an inner joy, an inner bliss, right in the inmost recesses of our heart, and this inner bliss we get only when our aspiration is genuine and sincere. We may get some mental and vital joy just because we are practising the spiritual life. But the real inner joy we get only when our aspiration is true and genuine. When we have inner joy, we see and feel that we are consciously sitting and growing in the Lap of God. The more we live in the world of higher aspiration, the more convincing will be our feeling of oneness with God. When we become consciously one with God, at that time He will stand right in front of us even when we are doing the most ordinary things.

If anybody wants to know whether his aspiration is genuine and whether he is really marching towards the Goal or not, then I wish to ask that person to observe his mind and heart. If in his mind he feels inner joy and peace and if his heart is flooded with joy and delight, not pleasure, then his aspiration is true and genuine. At that time the aspirant will know that he is not deceiving himself.

Is it necessary for us to aspire with something specific in mind, such as strength or some other divine quality?

Sri Chinmoy: No, your aspiration has not to be specific in that way. Aspiration must not come from the mind. Please do not think that you have to aspire for peace, for strength, for anything specific. If the mind dictates to you, its message will be all wrong. The mind will immediately tell you to pray for a thousand and one things at a time. But aspiration is something spontaneous. It comes directly from the heart.

In the morning, or any time when you start your meditation, a spontaneous feeling will come from your heart. This feeling will compel you to pray for something or to invoke something. This feeling does not operate through the mind.

Why do some people not aspire?

Sri Chinmoy: In the spiritual life we use the term "inner awakening". If one is awakened, then naturally that person will run towards his Goal. When you are ready, when your hour has struck, you will get up and run towards your Goal. Then after a while somebody else will be ready and he will run towards his Goal. The spiritual life is not like the military life where all are forced to go in the same marching formation. No! There is no compulsion; there is no force. The spiritual life is voluntary; it is a matter of your own choice. Accept God or reject God at your own sweet will.

But we have to be wise. If we accept God, then we feel that sooner or later we will really be fulfilled. If we do not consciously accept God today, then there will come a time when He will compel us to accept Him because He will not allow us to remain unfulfilled and unrealised; for the very purpose of God's creation is fulfilment.

I will tell you a story. Two sons are standing in front of a lake and the mother is observing them. One son is very good and obedient; he wants to please the mother. He knows that if he goes into the water his whole body will be refreshed; he will have a sense of purity. So he jumps into the lake and he is clean and fresh. But the other son is lazy. The water is very cold and he is afraid of it. He is waiting, waiting, waiting. The mother waits for some time, and then she gets annoyed and just pushes him into the water.

The first son was obedient and knew the necessity of taking a bath, so he did. In the spiritual life also, those who are awakened – the obedient children, the spiritual children – will naturally do what is necessary to please their Inner Pilot, God. They know that by pleasing their Inner Pilot, they are accelerating their Godward march. Others who do not feel the necessity, who are afraid and reluctant, will keep

God waiting for a few years, a few hundred years or a few thousand years. Then God will compel them because God, like the mother, knows the necessity of cleaning, purifying and illumining the soul.

The spiritual life is not like a race, where everyone starts at the same time and from the same starting point. When you are ready, you will have your starting point; when I am ready, I will have my own starting point. But the Goal is always the same. You may start your journey a few hours or a few years ahead of me, but when you reach your destination and when I reach my destination, it will be the same place. But this is true only if it is the ultimate, the highest Goal. Otherwise, your goal may be just to have an iota of Peace, Light and Bliss. So, when you have come to that place, you are satisfied and you don't want to have anything more. On your way to the ultimate destination you will reach some partial goal and perhaps think that this is the final Goal. Then you will stay at your goal for some time, because your inner or outer being does not want to go farther, higher and deeper. But when I reach that goal, which I will also have to attain, I may want to go farther. While you are walking down the street you see a beautiful tree with flowers and fruits. You stop and enjoy the fruit and think you have reached your Goal. But on my way to the Goal I may say, "No. There is something more beautiful, more powerful, more meaningful than this." Then naturally I will go farther and cover more distance. When I reach my goal, I will see that it is not a mango, but a diamond and at that time I will be satisfied. You will also go higher and farther after reaching your goal, because the ultimate Goal has to be won. But when I reach my *ultimate* Goal and when you reach your *ultimate* Goal, it will be the same, for everyone's ultimate Goal is the same.

Why is it necessary to have flowers, candles and incense in order to meditate?

Sri Chinmoy: When we keep our physical body clean and pure, when we offer flowers at our shrine, when we burn candles and incense, these things give us an additional opportunity to convince our physical mind that we are doing something most significant. But this is not the ultimate reason. The ultimate reason is to make ourselves constantly aware of our inner aspiration, the mounting flame within us. Then constantly we have to fly within to our highest level of consciousness.

What role does sincerity play in one's aspiration?

Sri Chinmoy: I will tell you a story. Once upon a time there was a king who ordered his subjects to dig a pond. Then he said, "There will be no water in this pond. It will be filled only with milk." So he told all his subjects to bring a jug full of milk the next day.

Now the following day, a brilliant thought flashed across everybody's mind. They thought, "Let me take a jug full of water to fill the pond. Others will bring milk, so how will the king know who has brought milk and who has brought water?"

So everybody brought water. And when the king and queen went to see the pond in the evening, they saw it was all water; there was no milk at all.

Here also some of the disciples feel, "If I don't aspire, no harm. Somebody else will aspire. How will the Master know whether I am aspiring or not?" We can deceive an ordinary king by pouring in water instead of milk, but a spiritual Master cannot be fooled. A God-realised person will immediately be able to know who is aspiring and who is not aspiring. If there were four people sitting here in front of me, immediately with my occult vision I would be able to say, "He is aspiring: he is not aspiring."

With a spiritual Master there is constant forgiveness. A spiritual person will say, "Today he has come without aspiration. But let me forgive him. Let me show him my utmost compassion and tomorrow he will try to come with a real, sincere inner cry." The king would get angry with his subjects. He would say, "You people have all deceived me. I will punish you." But a spiritual Master, in spite of knowing that he has been deceived outwardly, will use only his forgiveness-weapon. He says, "If I can forgive this person, if I show him my compassion, then tomorrow he will make an attempt to please me. This time he will really bring milk and not water." This is what a spiritual Master does.

Sometimes I have an inner longing within my heart. What is the spiritual significance of this?

Sri Chinmoy: Longing itself is meditation. You cannot separate inner longing from meditation. Outer longing or desire for name, fame, money and material possessions is simply foolish. Inner longing is the cry for oneness with the Source. That is a form of meditation. You are a secretary. While you are typing, if you type most soulfully in order to become one with the Supreme in your spiritual Master or with God, that is real meditation. On the other hand, if you want to show that you can type better or more speedily than someone else, then that is not divine longing. Your longing has to be in the highest plane of consciousness. This is the longing that will make you feel one with the Supreme and with your Master. The longing that separates you from God but gives you outer success in various ways is not meditation. The longing that will consciously make you totally one with God is real meditation.

Will you please explain how it is that the soul evolves only on the planet Earth?

Sri Chinmoy: The soul manifests only on this planet because this planet is in evolution. Evolution means constant progress, constant achievement. When one wants to make progress, when one wants to go beyond, then this is the place. In other worlds, the cosmic gods and other beings are satisfied with what they have already achieved. They do not want to go one inch beyond their achievement. But here on earth you are not satisfied, I am not satisfied – nobody is satisfied with what they have achieved. Dissatisfaction does not mean that we are angry with somebody or angry with the world. No! Dissatisfaction means that we have constant aspiration to go beyond and beyond. If we have only an iota of light, then we want to have more light. Always we want to expand.

When the creation started, the souls took different paths. Those that wanted the ultimate Truth, the infinite Truth, accepted the human body so that they could some day possess, reveal and manifest the Truth here on earth. According to our Indian tradition there are thousands of cosmic gods. There are as many presiding deities and gods as there are human beings. These presiding deities and gods remain in the higher worlds, either in the vital world or in the intuitive world or in some higher plane. Right now, according to their limited capacity, they have more power than we have. But when we are liberated and realised, when we are totally one with the Supreme's Consciousness, with the Supreme's Will, then we shall transcend them.

Our human capacity is infinitely greater than that of the so-called presiding deities because they are satisfied, whereas we are not satisfied with what we have. But actually it is not a case of dissatisfaction; it is a case of constant aspiration.

We know that our Supreme Father is infinite. We feel that we have not yet become the Infinite, but we cry to expand, expand. This planet has that inner urge. On the one hand, it is obscure, it is ignorant, it does not care for divine life. But on the other hand, it has that tremendous inner urge of which most human beings are not yet aware. When the inner urge is functioning, then there is no end to our possibilities, no end to our achievements. And when we achieve the Infinite, then naturally we surpass the achievements of other worlds.

In the future, will people always have to aspire like us? Or at some point will people no longer be born on earth?

Sri Chinmoy: People will continue to be born and evolution will also continue. We are human beings right now, not animals. But we have so many animal qualities: we quarrel, we fight, we have wars, we do so many undivine things. We actually strangle one another with our hatred and jealousy. But again, we claim that as human beings we are a superior species, we lead a higher life. But in what way? When we enter into ourselves we see that we are human animals. Still, we have made a little progress. We don't want to remain ferocious animals. Among us, some people are really aspiring and crying for God. Eventually they will see the Truth and grow into the Truth. This is evolution.

We cannot say that after four hundred or five hundred years there will be no more animal or human incarnations. There *will* be animals, there *will* be people, but they will be more perfect. Now, out of ten thousand people, one person may aspire. But the time will come when it will be just the opposite. We will have made such progress that only one person out of ten thousand will *not* aspire.

We cannot say that there will be another type of evolution in which everybody will descend fully illumined to earth. No! I have worked hard for many years and centuries in order to realise God. Will someone else not have to work at all? Will God do everything for him immediately? No, everybody has to work. God's Grace descends only when we work hard, when we aspire most soulfully. True, some people realise God when they are in their teens. You may say, "Oh, I have been meditating for twenty or thirty years, while he has meditated only for five or ten years. How is it that he has realised God?" But you do not know that fifty or seventy years ago in his previous incarnation he meditated intensely for many years. Similarly, the world is now imperfect and only gradually, gradually will it become perfect. It is not that at a fixed time the Light will dawn and all non-aspiring people will suddenly run towards the Goal. No! Evolution is a slow, gradual process.

How long do we have to continue to reincarnate?

Sri Chinmoy: If one aspires, one expedites one's realisation. Otherwise, an ordinary human being takes hundreds and hundreds of incarnations before actual realisation takes place. Aspirants who consciously enter into the path of spirituality and try to discipline themselves on the strength of their inner cry will naturally gain their realisation sooner than those who are still sleeping and are not yet conscious of the inner life.

Now, after one realises God, if it is God's Will, that person need not take any more incarnations. If the person is tired, then he may say, "No, I don't want to be of any help to humanity; I only want to realise God. After realisation I would like to stay in some other plane of consciousness." But some realised souls will want to go back to the earth-consciousness and serve aspiring humanity. It all depends on the individual soul and on God's Will.

You said that a spiritual Master is a practical man because he wants to bring God to men. But is it practical for someone involved in the world to aspire?

Sri Chinmoy: The problem is that we have no conception of spirituality. We think that a spiritual man has to leave the world and live in a cave; otherwise, how can he be spiritual? But in real spirituality, man has not to leave the world in order to realise God. Where is God? God is inside your heart, inside everybody's heart.

A spiritual man should be a normal man, a sound man. God Himself is normal; He is not insane. In order to reach God, a spiritual person has to be divinely practical in his day-to-day activities. Spirituality does not negate the outer life. But we have to know that the outer life does not mean the animal life. The outer life should be the manifestation of the divine life within us.

When you spoke of the need to transcend the past, you said that the world is continually evolving. Could you say more about this?

Sri Chinmoy: The world *is* progressing. If we go deep within, we see that the world is really evolving. In the outer world we see fighting, battles, wars. But actually, when we say "the world", that does not mean the outer happenings. "The world" means our very own existence. Each person represents the world. If we are aspiring, then while going deep within, we can see in our own human nature that we ourselves need to make progress. We still have within us millions of silly, dark and hostile forces.

Now when we accept the spiritual life, we feel that we are no longer victims to those dark forces. Those who have accepted the inner life, the spiritual life, can feel their inner progress. The world around us may be all chaos, but we know that there is also another world, the inner world. In the inner world, we see the achievement of ever-transcending perfection.

Each person has to know and feel how much he has progressed. When he accepts the spiritual life and walks along the path of spirituality, he is bound to see inner progress. In the inner world he achieves Peace, Light and Bliss; but in the outer world his nature is still imperfect. It takes time to manifest these divine qualities in one's outer behaviour. If we look only at the outer activities, we will be disappointed. But if we go deep within, we will see how much Peace this person has already achieved. In the course of time, he will be able to manifest what he has inside himself. What we have within, we are bound to manifest either tomorrow or the day after.

So when I say the world is progressing or evolving, it is all the result of aspiration; we see it and feel it. At the same time there are many who are not aspiring and they may feel that the world is not evolving. When we aspire, we *do* see the evolution in our own nature and in others' lives. But if we do not aspire, we do not see this inner progress at all. Only in the world of aspiration does our inner progress and the progress of the world exist.

The world is evolving. Once upon a time we were all animals. Now we are no longer in the animal kingdom; we have progressed. We have now discovered the mind. But a day will come when we will be far more illumined than we are now. When we think that just a few centuries ago we were all animals, who knows what we are going to be four hundred or six hundred or eight hundred years from now? In the process of evolution, perfection is bound to dawn.

The spiritual life and the outer life are one. It has been said, "I walk slowly, but I never walk backwards." In the spiritual life also, one may either walk slowly and steadily or march fast, but he has to realise God. One may reach the Goal sooner than another, but all are moving forward towards the Goal.

How can our aspiration help us to appreciate the outer world?

Sri Chinmoy: God is the only Truth here on earth and there in Heaven. For the aspirant, God comes first. But that does not mean that he neglects or negates the world. No, far from it! He loves God. He loves humanity. He loves God because God is all Love. He loves humanity because inside humanity is God, the All-Love.

When we appreciate somebody's physical beauty, we are appreciating the outer beauty, which is infinitely inferior to the inner beauty. But if we can appreciate the inner beauty first, then we feel that the outer beauty can be appreciated in a divine way as the manifestation of the inner beauty. So when we appreciate outer beauty, we have to know that inside the outer beauty is the Supreme, the All-Beauty. We appreciate the outer creation because inside the outer creation is the inner creation, which is all joy, all harmony and all perfection.

An ordinary human being can never dare to possess true hope, true love, true inspiration, true aspiration, because according to him God is in Heaven or somewhere else. He does not feel the presence of God inside him, in front of him or around him. But a spiritual aspirant who is crying for God, who is constantly shedding soulful tears, trying to become one with God, feels that God is in the inmost recesses of his heart. He has not to go to the Himalayan caves in order to realise God. His God lives inside him. He feels that because God is inside him, God's creation also is inside him. A spiritual person always feels that God's entire creation is his home. God's entire creation is constantly being created and revealed with a new inspiration and a new aspiration inside the aspirant. He who has accepted spirituality in the truest sense of the term has first to feel that God is the sole reality. Then he will see that God's creation can never be separated from God.

What is the relationship between individual and collective aspiration?

Sri Chinmoy: Individual aspiration has to grow along with the collective aspiration. If one feels the need of realising God, this is his individual aspiration. With this aspiration he must enter into the collective world, because without entering into the collective world, he will have no existence of his own. His true existence lies in offering himself to the rest of the world. In the field of aspiration and in the field of realisation, individuality and collectivity must go together.

If a person is satisfied with his own state of consciousness and has no particular desire to improve it, is this a mistake or a violation of the rights of his soul?

Sri Chinmoy: There are two types of satisfaction. One type of satisfaction we see in the laziest fellow. He is satisfied; he won't budge an inch. Although he has many desires, he does not want to satisfy any of them. He is satisfied with sleeping and enjoying the world in his own way. In spite of the fact that he knows nothing, he has nothing and he will have nothing, he is satisfied.

But there is another type of satisfaction. One who is divinely satisfied says, "God knows what is best for me. He has given me what I actually need. I am praying, I am concentrating, I am meditating and He is helping me. I am happy with Him. I know it is His business to give me full realisation, infinite Light, at His choice Hour. I am satisfied with what I am and what I have, and at the same time I am trying my utmost to realise God. I am making this personal effort with my utmost love, devotion and aspiration, but at the same time I am satisfied with myself." This is the satisfaction of the true aspirant who does not demand anything from God.

The first type of person has no desire, nothing. He does not want to make any progress. He is in the world of ignorance. That satisfaction with living in ignorance and doing nothing is no satisfaction; it is stagnation. The other type of satisfaction comes when we are praying, concentrating, meditating, doing our best and all the time feeling that God is our all-loving Father. We know that He will give us what we actually need at His choice Hour.

Then there is a third category that is in between these two. Those who belong to this category go along the way and fulfil some of their desires and then become satisfied; they do not want to make further progress. They know that the destination is farther, but they have walked a bit and they are satisfied. They feel that it is too difficult to go to the end of their journey. So they stop for some time. Now from the strict spiritual point of view, these souls are not aspiring; they are dead souls. The souls of the lazy, idle human beings that are not aspiring and also those who have started the journey and then stopped either because of their laziness or because their goal seemed very far are dead souls in the spiritual life.

If one is aspiring consciously with the soul, the physical, the vital, the mind and the heart, then naturally the soul will be most grateful to that aspirant. But if somebody does not aspire at all, if he has never thought of the spiritual life or if he has stopped caring for the spiritual life, the soul has infinite patience. It will never be frustrated. The soul has taken the responsibility for the entire being, and the soul is ready to wait for thousands of years for the co-operation of the other parts of the being. But at times it happens that the Supreme puts pressure on the individual through the soul. We cannot delay indefinitely. The soul's patience is infinite, but there is a limit to its duration. If one goes beyond the limit and the soul feels that the time is absolutely ripe for the individual to aspire to go beyond his ignorance-life, at that time the soul takes action. It gets the sanction and Blessings from the Supreme to put pressure on the individual.

So these are the two kinds of satisfaction. There is no violation of the soul in the case of lethargic satisfaction, but we have to say that these are dead souls. There is violation in a mild way, but actually one cannot violate the rights of the soul. God's ultimate Truth can be violated by no one, although some individuals delay their own progress. Eventually everybody has to reach the Truth and achieve the Truth, but we can delay our achievement with our ignorance and then we will not go as fast as the aspiring souls. True, lack of aspiration is a kind of subtle violation. You are postponing your aspiration. But the real violation is never to accept the Truth; and that violation can never be committed. We have to accept the Truth either consciously or unconsciously. If we do not accept it willingly, then we will have to accept it under pressure.

You spoke of conquering desires and transforming desires into aspiration. How does one do this?

Sri Chinmoy: It is not only possible, not only practical, but inevitable. Each human being will transform desires into aspiration, either today or tomorrow. We are starting our journey with desire, but tomorrow we have to continue our journey with aspiration.

Your eldest and dearest son goes to school. Today you may pray to God, "O God, make my son stand first in the examination. How I wish that my son should be first!" This is your desire. But tomorrow you will pray, "O God, I do not want my son either to be first or to be last. I want him to be only what You want. Please give him true Wisdom, because You are Wisdom, You are divine Wisdom. He is my dearest son and I want him to have only divine knowledge, illumination. If You can give him illumination, I will be most grateful to You." In that way you are transforming your desire into aspiration.

When you desire something, you have to feel that at that time you are nowhere near your Goal. But when you aspire, you have to feel that the Goal is not elsewhere; it is deep, deep inside you. All your desires will be killed if you say only one thing: "Let Thy Will be done." If we want our human will to be fulfilled, then our aspiration immediately is dead. But in one prayer:

"Let Thy Will be done," we transform our desire into aspiration.

Do we lose our desires after realising God?

Sri Chinmoy: If you have realised God, then you have no need to desire anything. God is everything and God gives you everything. Normally we have thousands of desires. As soon as one desire is fulfilled, we have another to take its place. Our desires are endless. But true aspiration for God is not a desire. It is a flame from our soul which is rising up, taking the heart and the mind with it, trying to unite our entire being with God. True aspiration brings God's help and His Grace, whereas desires end only in frustration.

How can we best solve our problems?

Sri Chinmoy: We can solve our problems only if we know how to live the life of aspiration, the life of the soul. The soul is ever free. But when the soul enters into the body, as soon as we see the light of day, ignorance tries to envelop us. At that time fate starts its play.

It is our personal effort and God's infinite Grace which can change the face of our fate. A shoemaker's son becomes prime minister; a farmer's son becomes president; a beggar's son becomes a multi-millionaire. How? They have changed the face of their fate. What they needed was adamantine will. On the strength of our will-power we change our fate. Fate can be changed, is changed and must be changed by an unchanging will.

There are four significant spiritual words in Sanskrit: *dharma, artha, kama* and *moksha*. Dharma's literal meaning is virtue. If we follow an inner life of discipline and self-giving, then in our day-to-day activities we can acquire dharma.

Artha means wealth. It can mean inner wealth and it can also mean outer or material wealth. For an aspirant, artha is inner wealth; for an ordinary person, it is outer wealth.

Kama means desire. In the lowest sense it means the enjoyment of sex-life, but the root of the word is desire. As human beings we desire. When desire is transformed, it is called aspiration. Desire binds us, aspiration frees us. When we live in aspiration, we enjoy the Peace, Bliss, Light and Power of divine Freedom. When we live in desire, we bind and imprison ourselves every second, every moment of our earthly life.

The fourth word is moksha. Moksha means liberation. Liberation from what? Liberation from ignorance, liberation from limitation and imperfection, liberation from the past: this is moksha.

When we live in dharma, we cannot free ourselves totally from fate. Free will cannot embrace us at that time. When we live in artha, if we cry for inner wealth, then we are running towards the Infinite. But if we cry for material wealth, then we are binding ourselves constantly. If we live in the world of kama, then we will ask for one house, two houses, three houses; there will be no end to our hankering. Each time we desire, we enter into the futile world of nothingness. But each time we aspire for moksha, we free ourselves from the prison cell of ignorance and death.

How do I overcome the obstacles of ignorance?

Sri Chinmoy: How do you overcome ignorance? With your aspiration. Always try to cry inwardly to overcome ignorance-sleep. When you sleep you don't cry; but when you cry you can't sleep. When a child is really sleeping, he cannot cry; he has to awaken first. And when he is pinched with hunger and crying for nourishment, then he can't sleep. The outer cry is for name and fame; the inner cry is for Peace, Light and Bliss. If you can cry for Peace, Light and Bliss, then ignorance-sleep will automatically leave you.

Can anything stand as an obstruction to our aspiration?

Sri Chinmoy: Very often we see that death is an obstruction to the aspirant. Almost all souls, in spite of being very great and spiritual, forget their past achievements, past aspirations and deepest inner cry when they take a new incarnation. For twelve or thirteen years they remain in ignorance. Sometimes it happens that spiritual souls do not regain their past aspiration until the age of fifty or sixty. The fifty or sixty years during which these individuals have not been consciously aspiring are absolutely meaningless from the spiritual point of view. So in this incarnation they have lost fifty or sixty years and in their past life also their aspiration was cut short by death. That means that perhaps eighty years have been wasted. In this case death is a real obstruction.

Aspiration should be like a bullet. It should pass through the death-wall. Death is obstruction for the sincere aspirant who cries to realise God in this life here on earth. For non-seekers it will take hundreds or thousands of incarnations to realise God anyway. But for genuine aspirants who cannot live without God-realisation and who want realisation here and now in this incarnation, death is a real obstruction. We have to remove death's obstruction with our aspiration.

What can one do when one feels his aspiration fluctuating? At times I have a feeling of emptiness and nothingness.

Sri Chinmoy: First of all, you have to know that all spiritual figures have said that in our spiritual lives we have to go through a "desert". We cannot live on an oasis all the time. There are always dry periods. Not one spiritual figure on earth can claim that he has not suffered through these dry periods. When we cross this barren, empty desert we feel that there is no aspiration. However, we have to feel that aspiration *is* there, although right now we seem to be on an endless journey.

How can we escape from this desert? There are four different ways. In your case, let us say that every day your appointed time for meditation is six o'clock in the morning. But for the past two days you have been unable to go deep within or meditate sincerely, and now you are frustrated. At that time you should choose a spiritual book written by a realised soul or by a devotee who is full of devotion for his spiritual Master. Then, while reading the devotee's book, you will see your whole body become a flood of tears. You will shed tears, tears, tears of delight. To read any book written by a spiritual Master or devotee at the time of a dry period in our spiritual life is one of the most effective ways of returning to the zenith of our spiritual aspiration.

But what if you don't have a book written by an illumined soul or a devotee? What will you do then? The second method is to immediately go and mix with your brother and sister disciples. Being with your spiritual family will drive away those negative forces. With your brother and sister disciples you will have spiritual conversations. You will appreciate your Guru and God and how they have shown you such Love, Concern, and Compassion. In the beginning you may feel that you are such a hypocrite in saying, "Oh, I am now in a miserable condition and I am appreciating my Guru or God." But you will see that if you just start appreciating your Guru or the Supreme, immediately you will shed tears. These tears come directly from your soul. And your soul will then unite you again with your highest aspiration.

Now the third method for curing a dark, dry period in your life of aspiration is to repeat the name of God or the Supreme, or your Guru's name, or even your own name, if your Master has given you a spiritual name. The name that he has given you is the name of your soul. Just repeat the name and do not think of the meaning; only repeat it just like a child learning how to read or study. At that time he will repeat the lesson by rote without learning the meaning. In this way immediately the consciousness of your soul's name or the name of your Master or the name of the Supreme will enter into your entire body.

The fourth method is to keep a spiritual diary. During your spiritual journey, you have to write down notes of your soul-illumining experiences, visions and inner feelings. Today you are in despair, in darkest night. But two months ago you were in the brightest Light. You had a wonderful experience. You saw that Krishna was playing the flute right in front of you, or you saw a flood of Delight and your whole existence became a sea of Delight. These experiences should be recorded in your diary. As soon as you read your diary, your inner being will respond to the highest experiences you had two months ago. Then immediately the inner feeling, the inner joy, the soul's joy will drive away your despondent feelings of misery, loneliness and frustration. So whenever you have good experiences, high experiences, elevating experiences during your meditation, please write them down.

These experiences are actually the living breath of our existence. If we can recollect our highest and deepest experiences at the time of our frustration, then we will get immediate relief. These experiences are not based on falsehood. It is we who have had all these divine spiritual experiences and they will cure the disease which we have right now. Sooner than at once we shall be cured.

Sometimes when I sit down to meditate, it is very spontaneous; I don't have to do anything. But why is it sometimes so difficult to get into a meditative state?

Sri Chinmoy: First I wish to tell you that every day we cannot eat the most delicious food, although that is our wish. In the spiritual life also, especially in the beginning, it is next to impossible to have a most successful meditation every day. Even spiritual Masters have gone through dry periods in their inner life. So for beginners in the spiritual life to have this kind of experience is not at all blameworthy.

Now how is it that every day we cannot meditate well? We cannot meditate well because we do not renew early in the morning our love, our devotion, our surrender to the eternal Pilot in us. Every day the eternal Pilot feeds our inner hunger. For an aspirant, spiritual food is more necessary than material food. Still we do not offer our deepest gratitude to the Inner Pilot even for one second.

The divine secret is this: the very act of praying, of concentrating, of meditating is a great sign of divine Grace. So, early in the morning, before you start meditation, try to offer your gratitude in the form of love, devotion and surrender to the Guru, to the Supreme, to the Inner Pilot just because He has given you the aspiration to meditate. Aspiration comes first. Your meditation will be the result of the aspiration which the Inner Pilot has given you.

A time will come when you will not have to meditate; meditation itself will meditate for you. That is to say, after some time you will be one with the consciousness of meditation. Now you are crying to enter into the consciousness of meditation, but a day will come when meditation will be pleased with you. It will take care of your outer life and your inner life.

So, to come back to your question, every day before you start your meditation, offer your gratitude in the form of love, devotion and surrender to the Supreme. Then, I can assure you, not even one day will you fail to have a golden meditation.

Guru, sometimes when I have a very difficult problem I feel that I should do nothing before meditating on you or thinking of what you would like me to do. But at the same time I don't have the inspiration at that moment to meditate. What should I do?

Sri Chinmoy: When a difficult problem does not allow you to meditate, you have to feel that that problem is your real enemy. You do not allow an enemy to enter into your room. But if he has already come in, then either you have to push him aside or you have to call the police. If you are strong, if you have the power, then you can push your enemy aside. That is, you have to throw the difficult situation out of your mind. But if you see that your enemy is much stronger than you, then call the police. And who is the police? Here the police is my grace or the Grace of the Supreme. Just cry, "Guru, come, come to me with your grace and compassion!" The divine police will immediately come in the form of compassion. This compassion will throw the enemy out of your mind-room and solve the difficult problem.

In spite of the fact that we want inner realisation and inner light, we find it difficult to fight against outer disturbances. Why is that so?

Sri Chinmoy: First of all we have to know how much aspiration we have. If we have boundless aspiration – that is to say, our inner cry must be constant – then this aspiration will climb up while God's Grace descends. When our aspiration and God's Grace become one, detachment will play its role in our life. At that time we will feel that the outer world was disturbing only because we were seeing the outside world in a limited way.

A real spiritual person sees that the outside world is not something in a geographical area, but something in a plane of consciousness right inside his own being. When we see a stranger, we do not know whether he will disturb us, attack us or torture us. But when we see something inside us, we know it is ours and we have no fear. If we are aware of something divine inside us, then it becomes very easy for us to fight against all outside forces. Our aspiration burns away the outside forces of impurity and imperfection while at the same time it clears up all that is disturbing our inner consciousness.

There can be nothing more powerful than our aspiration. The very nature of our aspiration is to give us what we are actually striving for. Very often we confuse aspiration with desire. Aspiration is not desire. Far from it! Aspiration is something that wants to enter into the infinite Light, Bliss and Power. Desire wants only to grab, grab, grab and possess. Desire coming from the vital acts like a mad elephant, always breaking, always destroying. Aspiration is not like that. With aspiration we grow into the very thing that we want to achieve. And what do we want to achieve? Divinity, God the all-pervading Consciousness. The achievement of aspiration we cannot grab or possess. Only by entering into the all-pervading Consciousness and becoming one with this Consciousness can we grow into God's Light, Bliss and Power. This is what aspiration does.

The flame of aspiration has been kindled in you and it is burning most effectively. When you allow it to blaze fully, you will see that the outer world, the disturbing world, is actually deep inside you. Then the things that have to be burnt will be burnt and the things that can be transformed will be transformed. Aspiration will take care of all that. There is no other way to fight outer disturbances than to keep the flame of aspiration burning constantly.

My aspiration seems to take two forms. One is a dynamic cry and the other can best be described as a relaxed, peaceful kind of feeling. Which is preferable?

Sri Chinmoy: You have to know whether the relaxed feeling is actually your inner voice or a kind of lethargic feeling. Sometimes, after meditating for half an hour, people feel that they have done something remarkable. They think that they can relax for hours because they have played their role. But your inner cry must be constant and dynamic. Then after you have meditated for two or three hours the flow of dynamic aspiration will surcharge your entire being. Then, gradually you will get inner peace in the body, in the vital, in the mind and in the heart.

In the beginning you have to work hard. You have to struggle in order to cry constantly. But once you are in motion, there is no worry. When you want to drive a car you have to turn the key and do various other things. But when the engine is running, at that time you can relax. Similarly, in meditation you need the dynamic inner cry first. Then only can you get the divine peace and poise.

Now real spiritual poise is not a matter of self-deception. But inside us there are many forces that try to convince us that we have done something wrong. In your case, especially because you are a disciple of mine, I wish you to pay all attention to your dynamic inner cry. Your dynamic inner cry will lead you to your Goal. If it is the Will of God, then while you are marching or running towards the highest Beyond, God will give you a special message about the best type of aspiration for you.

When the aspirant feels that his spiritual progress has stopped and it is difficult to meditate, what should he or she do?

Sri Chinmoy: It is quite possible to get back that aspiration and there are various ways to do so. The first way is to repeat the name of your spiritual Master. Or if you do not have a Master, then you can repeat "AUM" or "Supreme". You should repeat the name while breathing in. There is no need of counting how many times you are doing it. You may repeat the name inwardly and silently as well as aloud. While you are breathing in, repeat it silently three times. You will be more than able to do this. Then you can repeat it aloud. From head to foot, make the word vibrate. This is one approach.

The second way to get back one's aspiration is to feel that it is just like a lamp. Let us assume that the wind has blown it out, so the flame is not burning any more. You need light. Now, who can give you light? One who has a burning flame of aspiration. So, when a particular aspirant is losing or has lost his aspiration, immediately he should go to another aspirant in whom the aspiration is ablaze.

Another secret is to compare the times when you had aspiration with this time when you don't have aspiration. When you had aspiration, what did you feel? And now that you don't have aspiration, what are you feeling? Try to see how many experiences you had at the time of your intense aspiration. Suppose one year ago I had intense aspiration. At that time twenty, thirty or forty higher experiences I had. Let me gather together all the experiences right in front of my mind, one after another. What vision did I have? Did I see the Light? Did I see an aura? Did I see another world? Did I see something else? All these experiences you have to bring back. While you are collecting your past experiences from the time when you had intense aspiration, you will see that those experiences are giving you a new life. The life that you have had for the last few months, which has been like a barren desert, will now be watered by the experiences that you had a year ago.

How can I increase my aspiration?

Sri Chinmoy: There are quite a few ways to increase one's aspiration. One very easy way is to mix with people who you feel have more aspiration than you have. In school if you mix with a better student, then naturally you will be able to observe why he is getting better marks than you are getting. He is studying hard or he knows some secrets; that is why he is getting better marks. Similarly, by observing how someone has disciplined his life, you can increase your aspiration. So always try to mix with someone who is one step ahead of you. That doesn't mean that you should look down upon someone who is inferior in your estimate. Far from it! You will show him your sympathy and love, but you have to feel that you can learn from the one who is above you. Again, that person will not be your ideal. Your ideal has to be only God or your spiritual Master. But you can try to see what good quality makes a person better than you.

This is not imitation; you don't have to be a carbon copy of anyone. You need not spend all your time thinking of how the other person is meditating, but if you see that an individual has increased his aspiration by meditating at four o'clock or five o'clock, then you will also be inspired to meditate early in the morning. Again, if you see that that person is doing better meditation because he has not yet eaten, then you will also meditate the next time without having eaten. These are some of the outer ways to observe the person who you feel is doing better meditation than you.

The inner way to increase your aspiration is always to feel the inner cry. You desperately need God-realisation. God-realisation is not theoretical; it has to be practical. You have to eat. You know that feeling oneness with others while they eat is not enough. You yourself have to eat. True, while others are eating you can feel that you are also eating. Otherwise, if somebody is eating and you don't have the capacity to identify yourself with that person, then you only feel jealous, frustrated and miserable. But identification is not enough. First you have to get the theoretical oneness and then you bring it to the practical level. Practical oneness means that you yourself have to eat. Then you try to feed others who are hungry.

In the spiritual life the best way to increase one's aspiration is to think of one's own Master twenty-four hours a day, if possible. You have to know that for you to think of your Master or meditate twenty-four hours a day right now is impossible. But for one or two hours you can read your Master's writings, for one or two hours you can mix with other disciples; then one or two hours you can spend speaking about your Master to friends who know nothing about him.

Very often by speaking about the Master to others you can increase your own aspiration. Suppose today you have no aspiration at all. If somebody who is an absolute beginner asks you something about your spiritual Master, then you have to speak. You are not fooling the person even if you have no aspiration at that time. You have to go deep within in order to see if you have any aspiration at all in your life. Immediately you will see that hundreds of times you have had the aspiration-cry. So you bring that aspiration forward. Then, while you are talking to that person, automatically your aspiration is increasing. Suppose today you don't have aspiration but just two days ago you had tremendous aspiration. Somebody has just read something about your Master in the newspaper and wants to know more about him. If you do not speak to that fellow because you are not aspiring and you are doubting your Master, then you are destroying your own possibilities. It is God inside this seeker who has come to you only to increase your aspiration. God is more concerned at this time about you. You have been sincere for two months or six months and just today your aspiration is low. So God out of His infinite Compassion is coming to you in the form of a seeker or a curiosity-monger so that He can again kindle the flame of aspiration in you. There are many ways to increase our aspiration when it is low. But the best way is to think only of the Master, to talk about him, hear about him, and read all his writings.

If your Master has written only one book, or even if he has not written any book but there is a book of his sayings, that book is more than enough for all the disciples who are following his path. If you say, "I have already read all my Master's writings," then you have to know that to read them once is not enough. You have to read and re-read them all. But one book may give you more inspiration than the rest. Now that particular book every day you should read. Some disciples read a book once and then say, "I have read it." If you read with your mind only, even though you read the same line both today and tomorrow, then you may not get any inspiration. But if you read with your heart, then from each word you will get boundless aspiration. Each day you will see new light in your Master's writings. From each word you will get new light. In India some seekers select one spiritual book and read it again and again. There are seven hundred couplets in India's gospel, the Bhagavad Gita. It takes three or three and a half hours to read and there are some people who read the book every day. Some seekers don't read any other book. They read this book again and again in order to be purified. And every day they are getting new inspiration, new aspiration from that book. Everyday you too can get new revelation. What is revelation? It is the fruit of your aspiration. So if you read your Master's writings, not as you read a newspaper, but with the feeling, "Today I am going to get new revelation," then you are bound to get it.

While you are working at your job you cannot read, or your boss will fire you. But if you at that time repeat the Supreme's name or your spiritual Master's name or if you visualise your Master, how will your boss know what you are doing? You are not deceiving your boss. Far from it! But you know that there is a superior boss and that is God. You may say, "How can I please two bosses?" I wish to say that if you satisfy the absolutely superior boss, God, then your salvation is assured. Naturally you have to perform your earthly duties. God has made one individual your temporary boss and this boss is paying you for your labour. With this money, you can stay on earth and lead a spiritual life, which is absolutely necessary. Satisfying your earthly boss is not undivine cleverness or shrewdness; it is wisdom. So you have to work six or seven hours a day for this boss. But during the rest of the time you can meditate, mix with other disciples, and read your Master's writings. In that way you can easily spend fourteen or fifteen hours a day in your Master's consciousness. If this is not aspiration, then what else is aspiration? A spiritual Master embodies realisation. If you are constantly knocking, knocking, knocking at his heart's door with your intense inner cry, then naturally he will come out and give you the key. How many hours a day are you devoting to him? If you spend only five minutes in his consciousness and the rest of your day is gone, wasted, then naturally it will take you longer to reach your goal. But when you are very devoted and surrendered, then you will see for how many hours and in how many ways you can remain in your Master's consciousness. Then your aspiration will increase. When aspiration bears fruit, realisation dawns.

For two weeks or so I may be in a high consciousness, but then my consciousness begins to descend. How can I sustain a high consciousness for an indefinite period?

Sri Chinmoy: First of all, I would like to tell you that you are not alone in your suffering. All spiritual aspirants, with no exception, have gone through these ups and downs in their spiritual life. Sometimes we feel that we are walking through beautiful green forests and meadows. But then we find ourselves walking through deserts in scorching heat.

Many spiritual Masters have also had such experiences before realising God, even though their standard is infinitely higher than that of the average aspirants. They sometimes have to experience these spiritual deserts. In the case of some Masters this spiritual dryness lasts for a short period, while for others it lasts for a long, long time. They have to journey millions of miles in the spiritual life. But sometimes, even when they are on the verge of realising the highest Truth, the darkest doubt eclipses their vision and they doubt the very existence of God.

Fortunately, the Divine Grace intervenes and saves them from a catastrophe. It does not allow them to fail in their mission.

Now, in your case, I wish to tell you that as a seeker, as an earnest aspirant, every day you must make it a point to meditate. Just as you eat every day to maintain your physical strength, in the spiritual life you must meditate every day, because meditation is your spiritual food. True, you may not get your highest meditation every day, but that must not discourage you. You may not meditate well for a time, but do not give up. You will see that, like a kite, you will again fly very high.

In the spiritual life we should always try to be wise. The thought, the idea, the feeling that is not helpful has to be discarded like a dirty or worn-out garment. When you don't have a good meditation, just forget about it. I always say that the past is dust. Try to throw the past aside as soon as possible. On the other hand, if you have a good meditation today, that does not mean that tomorrow you have to think of today's meditation. By doing that you are again relying on your past. Instead of thinking of your previous meditation, even a good meditation, you will make better use of your time if you pay more attention to your future self-discovery. If you start your meditation by thinking of the wonderful, significant meditation you had on the previous day, you will experience joy. But at that time you have to know that you are withdrawing the money that you have deposited in your inner spiritual bank instead of adding to the amount.

When you start your meditation, try to go deep within and feel that you exist only for one person on earth and that is God. In the spiritual life, there should be someone whom you can call your dearest and that is God, the Supreme. The Supreme has to be dearest not only to the end of our life, but through Eternity. Every day if you can increase your faith in God, then every day you are bound to have your best meditation.

Why do some people seem to have their best meditation every day? The main reason is that they renew their faith, love, devotion and surrender to God every day. Love, devotion and surrender is my path. Some people will say it is inscribed on the tablet of their heart. But that won't do. Every day you have to write it afresh with golden letters. Every day you have to feel that you are making a new attempt. The day you entered into the spiritual life, you offered your existence to God. But that offering was not complete and even today's offering is not complete. If you feel that your offering is complete today, tomorrow when you go deep within you will laugh at yourself and feel that you are far from perfect. But either tomorrow or in the near future or in the distant future, this offering is bound to become complete. Again, there is no end to our progress, no end to our achievement.

I wish to tell you that you *can* prevent depression in your meditation. You can have a feeling of achievement, a feeling of accomplishment from your meditation if you renew your love, devotion and surrender and think of God every day. Try to wear a new dress within yourself. Every day you wear a nice, clean dress to satisfy yourself and to satisfy the outside world. It is necessary and obligatory to do so. Similarly, in the inner world also it is obligatory to wear gold, blue, pink, white and green. When we wear blue, we enter into Infinity; when we wear green, we enter into dynamic new life; when we wear gold, we enter into the highest realisation and manifestation. Every day please try to wear an inner dress inside yourself. When you are wearing an inner dress, you will see that all your love, devotion, surrender and other divine qualities are bound to come to the fore. Then you will become a fresh flower, a flower of inner beauty, inner divinity and transcendental reality. You will see that every day is bound to give you progress. Every second will come to you with the message of progress and inner success. So please try from now on to renew all your divine qualities each day, early in the morning. You will then see that there can be no clouds in your inner sky. It is all sunshine.

How can my aspiration be stronger and purer?

Sri Chinmoy: In your case, your aspiration is strong, it is pure. But now let us come to the comparative degree: you want to make it stronger and purer. I wish to say that you have to be strong and you have to exercise your inner freedom. When you exercise your inner freedom, your aspiration will automatically become stronger and purer. Right now you are not exercising your inner freedom. But if you know that something is good for you, really beneficial for your life, at that time you need not and must not have any fear.

There are many things which you know are absolutely good for you, but you are afraid of what others are telling you. You are listening to the members of your family. You have surrendered to others' wills and not to your own will, that is, to your soul's will. You have to do what you feel right from within, what comes directly from the Supreme within you. Right now you feel, "If I say this to my father or mother, then I won't be able to go to school; they will throw me out of the house." But when you take this attitude, then you are not using your own will. You have to say to yourself, "Whose child am I? God's child. Why have I to think of my human parents?" I am not saying anything against the human parents. But when you are determined to do something for God, the Supreme, then even if you are only thirteen years old, you can and you must exercise your own power.

You say that you are living in a land of freedom. Very often people use their limited freedom to lord it over one another. But when they have to use their own inner freedom to become something, to grow into something, to bring to the fore their own divinity, at that time most of them are silent. I am not saying that children have to fight against their parents. But when you are convinced that you are doing the right thing, when you are absolutely sure, at that time you must not surrender to the will of your parents. Although they are older than you, you have to know that God can speak through a child's mouth. The God within you is telling you what to do. In your case you are doing very well in your spiritual life. But if you want to do better, then use your will-power. I am your spiritual father. If you listen to God's Will within you, then I will meet with all the consequences to protect you, to save you, to show you new light.

Always be brave. Otherwise, today you will be afraid of an individual and tomorrow you will be afraid of a cat or a mouse or an ant. Fear is like that. When you are afraid of one thing, then before long you will be afraid of everything. But if you are not afraid of anything, then you won't be afraid of God. He is All-Powerful, but He is also All-Loving. Just because you know He is all Love, you approach Him. When you approach Him with love, you get His omnipotent Protection and everything else that He has and He is.

If you are afraid of ignorance in someone, no matter what the quantity, large or small, then you are surrendering consciously to the ignorance of that person. Then naturally his ignorance will enter into you. And ignorance itself is bondage. You may think, "Perhaps I did the wrong thing. What do I know? I am young." But just because you are a seeker, you know better than others. It is not your arrogance or stubbornness that is telling you this. You definitely know what to do because the soul within you is giving you the message of reality. The soul is all light, all illumination. When the soul tells you what to do, you have to feel that that is the *only* thing to do. So be brave inwardly; then strength is bound to come, purity is bound to come. If there is no strength in sight, then ignorance will devour us. Be brave, be brave.

How can one increase one's inner drive, one's aspiration?

Sri Chinmoy: There are various ways to increase one's inner drive or inner urge. If one is absolutely a beginner, if he has just entered or he is eager to enter into the spiritual life, then the first thing he has to do is to pray to God. What kind of prayer should he do? Prayer should be very simple, very sincere and spontaneous. Prayer is most effective in the early stages of the spiritual life because it is prayer that will increase the inner urge of the budding seeker. At the beginning when a person is just curious or only a little bit sincere in his spiritual activities, then we cannot call that person a seeker. But if one is about to jump or has already jumped into the sea of spirituality, if his spiritual life is certain, then we can say that he is a real seeker. The term "inner urge" or "inner drive" applies only to an aspirant.

Now if one is a step ahead in the spiritual realm, then he has to feel the necessity of God and the necessity of the fulfilment of God's Will on earth. The seeker knows that God has to be fulfilled on earth and he wants to take a conscious part in fulfilling God's creation. He is not satisfied with the rest of the world and he is not satisfied even with himself. If he wants a better creation in himself and in the world at large, then God is bound to give him an additional inner urge.

Then there comes a time when he feels that he can exist without anybody, without anything, but not without God. When the aspirant has that kind of inner conviction – that he does not need mother, father, brother, sister, wife, husband or anything, only God – at that point he has to be very careful. He has to see whether God wants him to make this kind of sacrifice or not. Just because he loves God more than he loves the rest of the world or humanity, it does not mean that he has to deny his nearest and dearest ones. No! Here in the field of manifestation he has relatives whom he calls dearest and who also call him dearest. If it is the Will of God that he should sacrifice everything, then he can sacrifice even his very existence. If God demands that he give up his so-called nearest and dearest ones, then he has to feel that his nearest is God, his dearest is God and nobody else. But God does not want him to leave his family and friends. God wants him to see the Divine inside everyone, inside his dearest friends, inside the members of his family. But at the same time he has to be prepared at any moment to give up everything if God wants him to do so. Then he will immediately run towards God, towards the ultimate Truth. If the seeker has that kind of surrendering attitude towards the fulfilment of God's Will, then God is bound to increase his inner drive in infinite measure. In your case also, I wish to say that if you can have this divine attitude, then God Himself will give what you want for your life.

Now I wish to speak generally in answer to your question about how one can increase one's inner drive. One can do it just by accepting the life of sincerity, the life of dedication, the life of absolute surrender. If one has a Master then he has to be absolutely sincere, absolutely dedicated and absolutely surrendered to the Master. Sincerity is his safeguard. One must have dedication to the Master and this dedication has to be total and complete. One must have surrender and this surrender has to be eternal and unconditional. If one has this kind of sincerity, dedication and surrender, then automatically, spontaneously, his inner drive is bound to increase, his aspiration is bound to increase.

Guru, how can we increase our aspiration and keep it steady?

Sri Chinmoy: To keep your aspiration high, steady and constant, three things are required: faith in yourself as a seeker; constant faith in your Master's judgement; concern for *what* is done, not who does it – that is, has the task been accomplished? Who accomplished it is not the question.

In your case, you have faith in me in abundant measure, but you do not have as much faith in yourself as you should have. If one does not have enough faith in oneself, then it is extremely difficult to maintain the purest or highest type of faith in the Master all the time. The purest and highest type of faith in the Master has to be continuous and constant; and for that one has to have complete faith in oneself. One has to feel, "I am destined to manifest the Master. I am destined to take continuous part in the Master's cosmic *Lila*."

Then every day you have to see whether the needful is done, not who has done it. Unfortunately, when we see that a particular individual has accomplished something, we feel as if we had nothing to do with it. You may say, "Oh, the Supreme has appointed him to do this and not me. I am worthless. I am useless. I cannot do anything." Then immediately you start criticising yourself and belittling yourself, which is wrong. If a fellow disciple has done something divine, then please feel that you yourself have done it. Your aspiration is equally responsible for his manifestation of the Divine. When something is manifested, if you feel that your aspiration had something to do with it, then you maintain tremendous aspiration. Each individual seeker should feel when something is achieved on the physical plane that he or she is equally responsible for the divine victory. Our joint victory lies in the manifestation of the highest aspiration.

Early in the morning when you start meditating, try to make yourself feel just for a minute that today you will be able to manage without eating a morsel of food, without drinking even a glass of water – that without eating or drinking anything at all you will be able to survive for a day, even for a week. But you must feel that if you do not aspire well, if you do not meditate well, then in the evening death will come and capture you. Death means the destruction of your aspiration, not the physical death. Annihilation will capture your aspiration if you do not meditate well. If you take your morning aspiration very seriously, then automatically your aspiration will remain high. Always give aspiration its due value.

Then a tremendous power will come out of you. The thing that determines whether you live or die is your aspiration and not your material food. You have to feel that aspiration is responsible for your earthly evolution and your heavenly achievement. When you are wanting in aspiration, you don't exist. Aspiration is the only reality in your life. With this feeling, automatically you will be able to maintain your highest aspiration twenty-four hours a day.

Notes

p.3: Sri Chinmoy answers questions about aspiration asked by seekers and disciples of the Master during the six years prior to 1974.

Aspiration and God's Hour

I – Meditation

What does it mean to meditate?

Sri Chinmoy: Meditation means conscious self-expansion. Meditation means one's conscious awareness of the highest Reality. Meditation means the recognition or the discovery of one's own true Self. It is through meditation that we transcend limitation, bondage and imperfection. First we face these limitations, then we transform them and finally we transcend them. So meditation means the discovery of one's own highest transcendental Reality.

Can you reveal the inner secrets of meditation to me?

Sri Chinmoy: Yes, I can, provided you accept me as your spiritual guide and I am in a position to accept you as my student. The disciples whom

I have accepted will definitely see the divine Light with my inner assistance and under the express guidance of the Supreme, who is my Guru, your Guru and everybody's Guru.

Guru, you have talked about meditation many times, but it still seems like a very vague word to me.

Sri Chinmoy: Indeed, meditation is a vague word. We use it in season and out of season. What does meditation mean? Meditation means the language of our inner life and the language of God. It is through meditation that we can commune with God. It is through meditation that we can see God face-to-face. It is through meditation that we can know that God is both with form and without form.

Each person has to have a meditation of his own. He has to get it from the inmost recesses of his heart or from a spiritual teacher. In this university you have many teachers and each one is competent to teach you a particular subject. In the same way, if you want to launch into the inner life of aspiration, the life of the soul, then you will need a teacher who can teach you to concentrate, meditate and contemplate. Until you get a teacher, you may not be sure what message your inner voice is giving you.

You can start by reading scriptures and spiritual books. These books will instruct you how to discipline your life to some extent. But if you want to go to the end of the road and reach your inner Goal, then you need true meditation.

What is the relationship between concentration, meditation and contemplation?

Sri Chinmoy: In our spiritual life we start with concentration, then we enter into meditation and finally we enter into contemplation. When we want to develop will power, we concentrate. The mind is restless; constantly it moves from one idea to another. It cannot think of one thing for more than a fleeting minute. In concentration we focus only on one particular object or subject. We do not allow anything else to enter into our mind. If we know how to focus our concentration on a particular spot or on one of our chakras, we can concentrate on this. Through concentration we will be able to throw aside the many uncomely thoughts and undivine ideas that are in the mind.

Concentration acts like an arrow in the spiritual life. If doubt enters into our mind, the power of concentration will tear doubt to pieces. If fear enters into our mind, the power of concentration will chase away our fear. Concentration clears the way so that the traveller can walk along the path of meditation. How can we develop the power of concentration? We can develop concentration by leading a disciplined life, a pure life. Of course, if the seeker has a Master, the Master will be able to surcharge the seeker's life with the power of concentration. If we are concentrating on our Master, the Master is the only thing in our existence. At that time, nobody else exists for us. We don't look forward, backward or upward. Only the Master is in our mind. This is concentration: one-pointed attention on a particular thing.

When we have become successful in concentration, we enter into the domain of meditation.

When we enter into meditation, we try to receive inner peace, light and bliss. Meditation is a vast realm. There we try to enter into the reality which is called peace, light and bliss. Concentration focuses on a very small thing, but meditation deals with the vast.

When we meditate, we enter into the vast sea, the vast sky, and the reality of that vastness enters into our meditation. In meditation we see the whole sea all at once, whereas in concentration we take it drop by drop.

In contemplation we again go one step further. In contemplation we enter into the reality and the reality becomes part and parcel of our life. When we meditate on the sea or the sky, we enter into the consciousness of that vastness. But when we contemplate, that consciousness becomes our very own. So contemplation is the last stage. We start with concentration, then we enter into meditation and finally we go to contemplation. Contemplation offers us the message of oneness. The divine lover, the God-lover, becomes inseparably one with his supreme Beloved. The seeker becomes inseparably one with

God. Vision becomes inseparably one with Reality. The seeker and the Truth become inseparably one in contemplation. The finite becomes inseparably one with the Infinite. A tiny drop enters into the ocean and loses its individuality and personality and becomes the ocean itself. Inseparable oneness with the highest Absolute we get from contemplation.

After we have finished meditating, how do we go about contemplating?

Sri Chinmoy: At this stage of your life you need not do contemplation. Contemplation comes after quite a few years, when one is very advanced in the spiritual life. Contemplation is the highest rung of the ladder. First comes concentration, then meditation and finally contemplation. Here among my disciples, only very, very few have the capacity of limited contemplation; otherwise, all are up to the meditation state. The contemplation state is a very high state. Even those very, very few who do have the capacity to contemplate cannot do so at their sweet will. So in your case, please only think of meditation right now. Contemplation will take some time. When the time for contemplation comes, I will tell you.

Contemplation is required before God-realisation, so it cannot be ignored or avoided. But, in your case, the necessity for contemplation has not come, because your concentration is not yet perfect, your meditation is not yet perfect. When your concentration is perfect and your meditation is perfect, at that time also your contemplation will have to be perfected. Then you will be able to climb up these three rungs in the ladder of self-realisation. Then you will really be able to enter into the Highest. But now the time has not yet come for you to learn contemplation.

How can we tell which message we hear during meditation is the right one?

Sri Chinmoy: During meditation our heart gets the real realisation of Truth. Absolute realisation is something different, something far beyond this kind of awareness; but let us use the term "realisation" to describe the experience of the heart. After we stop meditating, our mind immediately tells us something else. It says, "No, this message cannot be right." The mind has its own realisation, which it thinks is better and more profitable than the realisation of the heart. But it may be that the realisation which seems to be the less profitable of the two is actually the higher realisation.

The heart always offers the same message. When we sit down to meditate in the morning, it gives one message. In the evening when we meditate, we will again get the same message from the heart. But in the case of the mind, one moment it says one thing and the next moment, as soon as we turn our head, it says something else. One moment the mind will say, "He is a good man. Last night he appreciated me in front of some people." But the next moment our mind remembers the past. Even though the past is now irrelevant, the mind remembers it. Then it says, "He is a rascal. He lied to me twenty years ago." So let us always listen to the dictates of the heart.

Why is meditation so spontaneous one day and the next day not?

Sri Chinmoy: Meditation needs practice. You have to practise to become spontaneous in your meditation. Why is it that you get hungry one day and the next day you don't get hungry? If you work hard on the outer plane, then you are bound to become hungry. If, on the physical plane, you run quite a few miles, then you are bound to feel hungry. Similarly, if you work hard on the inner plane, then you will be blessed with receptivity. In the inner plane, if you cry soulfully and devotedly, then you can create receptivity, and inside that receptivity you will feel gratitude. When you feel gratitude, at that time your meditation is bound to be spontaneous. So there are many ways to get hungry. But the ultimate cause of inner hunger, the real source of your inner cry is God and nothing else.

How can one overcome a feeling of hell and doubt when one meditates?

Sri Chinmoy: First of all, if our meditation is soulful, we cannot experience hell and doubt. But if our meditation is not soulful, how can we overcome a feeling of hell and doubt? First of all, we must have a fondness for meditation, a liking for meditation. Some people meditate in a mechanical way. They take it as a routine, as something imposed on them. But nobody can impose meditation on us. We have to accept it on our own. Very often people get bitter experiences and frustrated feelings during their meditation. Why? Because they do not like or love meditation. They simply feel that from meditation they will get something special, something unique. They are like beggars who think that by begging they will be able to become millionaires overnight. Very often when a seeker enters into the spiritual life he thinks that his entire existence will be inundated with peace, light and bliss overnight. But everything takes time. One cannot become a millionaire overnight;

one has to work hard. One cannot get a Master's degree in one day or in one year. One has to pass through kindergarten, primary school, high school, college and university.

So why do we have the experience of hell and doubt during our meditation? Because we are pulling and pushing. We are pushing ourselves beyond our capacity and we are pulling in something beyond the capacity of our receptivity. Our receptivity is very limited. We are trying to pull in something which will break the vessel within us. Or we are pushing ourselves beyond our capacity. We do not have the capacity to run, but we are pushing ourselves like the fastest runner in the world. Even though we do not have the capacity, we feel that by running we will reach the Goal. True, we have to reach our Goal, but if we run beyond our capacity, we will only fall and break our legs. Then our spiritual life will end.

We are experiencing doubt because we are not following the spiritual path systematically. We doubt humanity, we doubt God or we doubt ourselves. A seeker often feels that he will never realise God. Either God does not exist for him or he feels that he will not realise God because he is not pure enough, sincere enough or disciplined enough. But he is wrong. If the son exists, then the Father exists. If the seeker was created by God, which is absolutely true, then the creation is bound to reach the Creator. As the Creator can at any moment enter into the creation, so too the creation, with its sincere inner urge, can and will enter into the Creator.

Unfortunately, many people cherish a wrong idea called hell. There is no such thing as hell; it is only limitation, bondage. We are now experiencing the finite. Unfortunately, we have not yet experienced the Infinite, the Immortal and the Eternal. Just because we have not yet felt the Infinite, we feel that the opposite – the finite – is hell. But we have to know that the bondage that we are experiencing every day is only a passing phase. It is like an overcast day. For half an hour or for a few hours the sun does not shine, but finally the sun comes out. Each individual has an inner sun. This inner sun is now covered by fear, doubt, worries, anxiety, imperfections and limitations. But a day will come when we will be able to remove these clouds and then the inner sun will shine brightly.

If we believe in hell, then we are only belittling our own inner potentiality. We are all God's children. For us there is no hell; there is only light. But if we do not see the truth in the way that the truth has to be seen, then there is inner pain. This pain is bound to occur every day in our life. The truth is there, but we have to see the truth in the proper way. Then only will we see that life has its true meaning.

When we meditate, we must not expect anything from our meditation. God is meditating in and through us. The very fact that we want to meditate should please us. Millions of people are not meditating; they are wallowing in the pleasures of ignorance. How is it that out of millions and billions of people, we are ready to meditate? God has chosen us. The very fact that we are meditating means that we have been blessed by God. Here we have to know that He who has given us the capacity to meditate will also give us the result. But there is something called

God's choice Hour. Just because we have started meditating, we cannot expect peace, light and bliss overnight.

We have to feel that we are divine farmers. We cultivate the land and sow the seed. Then we have to wait for rain, for the divine Grace. A farmer does not get a bumper crop in a day. Similarly, a spiritual seeker will not get the bumper crop of God-realisation in a single day. If he wants to do this, then he is pushing himself beyond his capacity or pulling something beyond the capacity of his receptivity. He will naturally be frustrated and his frustration he will call hell. He must wait for God's choice Hour and remain satisfied with the idea that God will give him the capacity to meditate at His choice Hour. Patience is necessary. God has given us the capacity to meditate, so we should be grateful that He has chosen us and not anybody else right now. Then we have to wait for God's choice Hour. If we pull, if we push, then frustration will appear; and in frustration we will feel hell. We will doubt our own spiritual capacity and God's existence. So if we meditate for God's sake and not for our own sake, then we will never have doubt or this feeling of hell.

How does one bring the mind under control?

Sri Chinmoy: You have to know that we are the possessors of two rooms. One room is known as the heart-room; the other is known as the mind-room. The mind-room is right now obscure, unlit, impure and unwilling to open to the light. The heart-room is always open to the light, which is the light of the soul. We have to try to remain in the heart-room as long as we can. Finally there will come a time when our entire being is surcharged with inner light. When this happens, only then can we safely enter into the mind-room. But right now, if we enter into the mind, we will be totally confused because it is all darkness. We will be caught there; we will become a victim to the ignorant, undivine and suspicious forces of the mind.

We should not try to enter into the mind-room in the very beginning of our spiritual journey. To enter into this room we need abundant inner courage, inner light and inner assurance from our Inner Pilot. Very often we make a Himalayan blunder: we enter into the mind-room just because we see that it is all confusion and darkness, and we want to illumine the mind. But we have to know whether we have the necessary light at our command. If we have the necessary light, then we can enter into the mind-room and illumine it. But if we don't have enough light right now, then we have to enter into the heart-room where there is abundant light. Here we shall meditate and energise ourselves with the inner light of the soul. Then we will enter into the mind-room and illumine it.

So the most effective approach is to remain in the heart-room and not in the mind proper. I tell my students first to strengthen their inner life, their life of aspiration. They must bring to the fore their inner light, their soul's light, which is available most powerfully in the heart. If we concentrate on the heart, then sooner or later the light of the soul is bound to come to the fore. We will feel that we are in full possession of our inner light and that we can use it at our own sweet will. At that time, we can enter into the mind-room to illumine it.

How can I tell if I am meditating too much?

Sri Chinmoy: How can you tell if you are meditating too much? It is very simple. If you are meditating too much, then you will get a kind of tension or pain in the third eye. Also, if you are meditating too much – that is to say, beyond your capacity – then you may get a kind of rigid attitude. You may feel, "I am so divine, so perfect, whereas everyone else is all undivine and imperfect. They are all insignificant creatures." If you are trying to pull down peace, light and bliss from above beyond your capacity, then you may no longer get any joy or satisfaction from your earthly activities. You may come to feel that this earthly existence of yours is useless and meaningless. If you get this kind of disgust or depression or ascetic feeling, and if you want to withdraw from the world, then you have to know that you are trying to meditate beyond your capacity.

Also, it may be that you are trying to meditate in the wrong way – that is to say, in a way different from the way your soul wants you to meditate. You may meditate, say, for only fifteen minutes, which is a short time for meditation; but if the form of the meditation is not correct for you, then you will feel tremendous tension in your forehead.

There are many ways to meditate. You can meditate on the heart or you can meditate on the mind by trying to silence the mind. You may feel that your mind is now your best instrument, your most developed instrument. But when you look at the mind, you see that it is restless, it is uncontrolled. The mind is subject to all kinds of absurd and undivine thoughts. You see that you are not getting any real satisfaction from the mind. If you want to meditate on the mind, you will try to stop all thoughts. When a thought comes, right away you just stab it and kill it. But this kind of meditation may create tension for you. Again, you may feel, "I shall let every earthly thought, like a mad elephant, enter into my mind. I will sit for hours and my mind will roam freely in the world of thought. Finally, like a child in the playground, it will become tired and enter into the world of silence. Then I will be able to do real meditation." But this approach your soul may also find unsatisfactory.

I am not saying that one particular form of meditation is right and another is wrong. What is right for someone else may be wrong for you, and vice-versa. It depends upon the needs of the individual soul.

How do we receive God's Grace?

Sri Chinmoy: God's Grace is always there, but how many people utilise it? God's Grace is like the rays of the sun. The sun is always there, but what do we do? We get up late. Instead of getting up at five-thirty or six o'clock, we get up at eight or nine o'clock. Then we do not get the blessing of the morning sun. And when we do get up, we keep the doors and windows all shut and do not allow the sunlight to enter into our room. In the spiritual life also, God's Grace is constantly descending, but we are not allowing the Grace to enter into our system. We have kept barriers between God's Grace and our own ignorance. Only if we keep our heart's door wide open can God's Light enter into our existence. God's Light means God's Grace. There is no difference between God's Grace and God's Compassion-Light.

God's Grace is constantly descending; this is absolutely true. So we have to empty our inner vessel every day and fill the vessel with God's Peace, Light and Bliss. We have to feel that God's Light is there all the time and is more than willing to illumine us. Then only we will be able to utilise God's Grace. Again, if we miss God's Grace, we should not be doomed to disappointment. Today we have not allowed the sunlight to enter into our room, but tomorrow again the sun will be there. In the spiritual life also, if today we have not allowed God's Grace to enter into us due to our ignorance, no harm. Tomorrow we must definitely be prepared for God's Light to enter into us.

I am giving a lot of importance to aspiring through music.

Sri Chinmoy: There is nothing wrong if you feel aspiration in your music. But you have to know how many hours you can think of your music. If you spend five hours, six hours, seven hours a day on music, then spend one hour or two hours, let us say, on spirituality. Music is also a form of spirituality; I don't deny it. But the height that you will achieve from meditation either you may not get or cannot get from your music. Music is an added help. From meditation you may get ninety-nine dollars of spiritual wealth and from music you may get one dollar. There are many things that will not give you even one dollar's worth. Music is ready to give you five dollars' or even ten dollars' worth. But the main eighty or ninety dollars' worth you will get from your meditation.

If I get creative ideas while I am meditating, should I accept them or should I just try to feel with my heart?

Sri Chinmoy: As soon as you get an idea, you should consider it as a blessing from the Supreme. Creation is realisation; creation is progress. Please take these creative ideas as your own progress. When you get ideas, you have to know that they are creations from another world which want to manifest on the physical plane. When your meditation is over, you should write down the ideas. Afterwards, you can elaborate on them.

At the end of meditation, I feel very good. Is there anything I should do with that feeling, or any way to utilise it?

Sri Chinmoy: Whatever you feel must be preserved. How can you preserve it? Only by offering gratitude to the Inner Pilot. Also, you must feel that what you have achieved is not enough. You must continue. If you have received or achieved a dollar's worth of peace, then you must try to get ten dollars' worth of peace. And if you feel that you have developed an inner muscle to receive, then you must continue strengthening that muscle. If you have strong muscles, you can do a few push-ups, but if you have stronger muscles, then you can do more push-ups. In this way you can develop a very strong inner physique.

Guru, how can we have a feeling of giving and not expecting in our meditation, especially when we receive a force from you?

Sri Chinmoy: During your meditation, just try to throw your inner and outer existence into my transcendental Consciousness. In the transcendental Consciousness, you do not have to think of anything. You just throw yourself into the sea. Then the sea will feed you with light, peace, bliss and power. But do not expect peace from there, or any particular divine quality. I want to give you something, but when you expect, with your expectation you are binding yourself and you are binding me.

Human expectation is very limited. Suppose you want divine peace. This is wonderful. But when you expect, immediately your mind acts. The mind creates some receptivity inside you and you feel that you have the capacity to receive what you are expecting. But first you have to know that the receptivity that you have in your mind or in the physical is very limited. If you do not expect, but only try to give, then the problem of receptivity comes to the Master. Because you are giving, the Master also wants to give. In order to give, he has to make the vessel; he not only has to make it, but he has to make it very large so that he can give the amount that he wants to give. At that time the Master is bound to give you everything in boundless measure and, at that time, he creates the receptivity in you to receive what he has to offer. So when you meditate, just throw yourself with your utmost aspiration into my Consciousness. Your utmost aspiration should be the feeling of oneness. Feel that you are entering into something which is your true self. You are not entering into a foreign element or foreign person; you are entering into your own highest.

Guru, are you bothered by noise and other disturbances when you meditate?

Sri Chinmoy: In silence we possess the highest. If I enter into my own highest trance, at that time nothing will bother me. But the moment we talk, we come down one level. There we see that the earthbound consciousness, the noise and everything else there, is affecting us. If I want to remain in my highest and if I don't want to care about what is happening all around, I can do that. But if I am to be of service to my disciples, then how can I all the time stay there? If somebody is drowning in the water, then naturally the person who is on the shore has to also enter into the water if he wants to be of help. So here also, if a spiritual Master wants to remain in his highest, he has the capacity to do so. But from the highest he cannot help humanity. The students cannot come up to his height, so he has to come down to the level of the students. So I come down to the level of my disciples and teach them how to meditate. If I want to remain in my highest, ignoring them, or if I don't want to be perturbed by the earthly circumstances, noise and so forth, I can easily remain in my highest. But that will not help my fellow beings and my disciples.

Should I meditate on my third eye?

Sri Chinmoy: Sometimes during meditation, individuals concentrate on their third eye. There is nothing wrong with an individual meditating on his third eye. Only you have to know how much preparation you already have. Suppose your third eye opens up untimely and you are not spiritually mature. If you see with your third eye that your mother is going to die tomorrow, you will die today with worries and anxieties. Or your third eye may allow you to see the past. Suppose you see that in the past you badly deceived someone. Now you are such a sincere seeker, but you will feel so miserable because of what you did in the past. You will say,

"I have deceived someone, so in this incarnation how am I going to realise God? I am such an undivine person."

But if you have inwardly prepared yourself through gradual meditation on the heart, then if your mother dies tomorrow you will simply say, "Oh, it is God's Will. After all, I have come to surrender my whole existence to God's Will. If He wants to take His daughter, it is His business." And if you had been a thief or a very undivine person in the past, so what? Before you were undivine and now you want to become divine. That is why you have accepted the path of aspiration. This is called illumination, and illumination will save you. If you have this kind of illumination, and it is a living experience in your life, then you can easily meditate on the third eye without any fear. But unless you have illumination as a living experience, it is dangerous to open the third eye. Any serious incident that you see in the future will kill you right in the present. And if you become aware of any unfortunate incident that took place in your past, you will feel extremely miserable and you will not have the heart to go forward.

That is why it is not advisable in the beginning to concentrate and meditate on the third eye. But when your inner being is developed, when you are fully mature and are able to cope with the situations of the past and of the future, then there is nothing wrong with meditating on the third eye. At that time you develop your own power and you make the fastest progress. But right now I tell the beginners not to concentrate on their third eye, because it only creates unnecessary problems.

When I meditate, I lose energy and get tired. Is it because I meditate too much?

Sri Chinmoy: No, it is not because you meditate too much. If you are losing energy while meditating, it means that your meditation is incorrect. If you meditate well, you will gain energy, not lose it. If you do the right thing, naturally you will succeed. But if you meditate in a wrong way, then the meditation fails its own purpose.

Your meditation, unfortunately, is not the way it is supposed to be. You are supposed to meditate on the heart or on your inner being. But you are meditating on the mind or in some other wrong place. That is your problem. Meditation is the only way to gain infinite energy, infinite light and bliss. But if the particular method you use every day is wrong, then, naturally, you will lose energy instead of gaining it.

How many times should we meditate per day?

Sri Chinmoy: If one follows the spiritual path, then one has to meditate at least once a day. This is obligatory; otherwise, it is useless to follow the spiritual path. It is better to meditate at least three times a day, but if it is not possible to feed your soul three times, then please feed it at least once. I am telling this to all of you. At least once a day you have to feed the soul. Feel that the soul is a little child, a divine child. If you don't feed the soul, then it will starve and your divine manifestation will be delayed.

So, if possible, you should meditate at least three times a day: early in the morning, at noon or during your lunch hour, and in the evening. Your morning and evening meditation should be for a longer time, that is to say, half an hour, and your meditation at noon should be for five or ten minutes. If possible, on some days try to meditate seven times for ten minutes or fifteen minutes each time. Seven is an occult number. It carries great significance. But this does not mean that you will only count the number of times and not how soulfully you meditate. You may meditate seven times a day, but it has to be done most soulfully. If you feel that you can meditate soulfully only once, early in the morning, then that is enough. You have to see your real capacity, sincerity, willingness and joy.

How long should one meditate? How long can one meditate?

Sri Chinmoy: It depends on the individual seeker. One athlete may practise running for half an hour while there may be another who can run for only two or three minutes. In the spiritual life also it depends on how far the seeker has advanced. There is no hard and fast rule that we have to meditate for ten or twelve hours. But if we can meditate soulfully and devotedly for one, two or even six hours, we should do it. We should continue to meditate as long as we can do it soulfully and devotedly. But if we meditate beyond our capacity, we will get headaches and have serious problems. Someone might force himself to meditate for twenty-four hours, but what kind of meditation will it be if he does not have the capacity? This will not bring about any satisfactory result. On the contrary, one may become insane.

The best thing is to meditate as long as we can without creating any mental disturbance or any difficulty in our spiritual life. It depends entirely on the capacity of the seeker. It is like developing a muscle. Today we may exercise and become tired after five minutes. After ten days we develop our muscles and we can exercise for half an hour or even more. In the spiritual life there is a spiritual muscle. This spiritual muscle is our inner intensity, our aspiration. How long and how sincerely we can cry for God is our inner muscle.

Is it better to keep your eyes open or closed when you meditate?

Sri Chinmoy: It is better to keep the eyes open. Otherwise, when you keep the eyes closed, very often you go to the other world, the world of sleep. You may think you have had the highest, deepest meditation, but you have only been unconscious. But if you keep your eyes half open, a little open, then you are conscious of the outer world and, at the same time, you are conscious of the inner world. In order to be alert and aware of both worlds, it is always good to keep the eyes a little open. Sometimes if you feel that for two minutes or five minutes you want to keep your eyes closed, there is nothing wrong with that. But if you want to meditate for an hour or two hours while keeping your eyes closed, then I am sorry, but you will only fool yourself.

Can one meditate any place, even if one is walking or driving?

Sri Chinmoy: Certainly one can meditate anywhere when one has acquired the capacity. When you become like me you can meditate any time – while driving, while running, while cooking. But right now you are only a beginner. You can meditate in your highest only when you are alone in your room or here at the Centre. You do not have the mastery over your meditation in other places. If you want to do your highest meditation while driving or doing some other serious, important job, you may have an accident because you are not yet an expert or an advanced seeker. While walking, if you try to remain in the higher world, you will jaywalk and then someone will come and take your life away. So I do not advise you to do it.

I would like you to meditate as much as possible, but you have to know your capacity. In the car you may do japa. For a short while repeat the name of the Supreme, who is my Guru, your Guru, everybody's Guru. Then wait a few minutes and do it again. In this way you are helping yourself spiritually, and not putting yourself in any danger. But when you become an expert in your meditation, you can do it anywhere. In the beginning, a dancer always makes mistakes. But once he becomes an expert, he can dance anywhere he wants to.

Right now it is advisable to see what kind of capacity you have. You have to learn how to do the highest meditation and, at the same time, know what is happening on the earth plane. That is why I ask people during meditation to keep their eyes a little open, so that they can go to the highest while they are retaining their conscious oneness with Mother Earth. Otherwise, they will go up and forget all about this world, and then they are useless here.

I want everybody to become an expert climber. Everybody has to learn how to climb up the tree and bring down the mangoes and share them. If you have the capacity only to go up but not to come down, then you will be stuck there. The best thing is to learn to climb up and climb down. Gradually, gradually you will develop your capacity and then you will be able to do your best meditation anywhere.

II – Light

What is the most important thing for the spiritual aspirant to bear in mind?

Sri Chinmoy: The spiritual aspirant should always bear in mind that he is of God and he is for God. Right now he may be a budding seeker, he may be a beginner; so for him God cannot be or need not be always a living God. Sometimes the aspirant will only be able to imagine God, and sometimes, in spite of his outer efforts, he may not feel the presence of God in himself, and sometimes he may even forget the existence of God. But he has to bear in mind that he has a Source and that Source is Light, boundless Light, infinite Light. He has been wallowing in the pleasures of ignorance for many years and he has not yet come out of ignorance. But he has to feel that his Source is not ignorance; his Source is Light and Delight. He is for that Source and he is making a conscious effort to return to his Source. While returning, he is manifesting God-Delight here on earth. Even now he is in ignorance to some degree, but he is always for God-Life and he is always for God-Light. If he can remember this, then he will feel a constant sense of satisfaction in his life. He will feel Light, more Light, abundant Light, infinite Light in his outer and inner life.

How should you meditate on a particular quality – for example, light?

Sri Chinmoy: To meditate on a quality, let us say light, first try to imagine what will happen when that quality enters into you. Try to imagine what will happen if light enters into you. The answer is that illumination will take place. Put illumination in front of your mental vision and feel that slowly, steadily and unerringly you are growing into illumination itself. In this way, imagination will give you the message of reality. Then you have to feel that this reality is nothing other than your true self, and that you have to grow into this reality.

Is it necessary to control the mind first in order to receive the divine Light?

Sri Chinmoy: If we want to control the mind with our human will, then it will be like asking a monkey or a fly not to bother us. The very nature of a monkey is to bite and pinch us; the very nature of a fly is to bother us. To try and control the mind directly is just like trying to straighten the tail of a dog; it is impossible.

The mind needs a superior power to keep it quiet. This superior power is the power of the soul. We have to bring to the fore the Light of the soul, which has unlimited power. In the outer world, when somebody is superior in strength or power, he tries to punish the inferior. But in the spiritual world, the Light of the soul will not torture or punish the mind. On the contrary, it will act like a most affectionate mother who feels that the imperfections of her child are her own imperfections. The heart will feel the obscurity, impurity and darkness of the mind as its own imperfections and, at the same time, the heart will be in a position to offer its Light to the mind. In pin-drop silence it will try to transform the nature of the mind.

What is the source of the higher Light?

Sri Chinmoy: This Light actually comes from the soul; it is inside us. The moment we can have free access to our inner being or to the soul, we will see that this Light is coming to the fore to permeate our whole outer existence.

How quickly does a mantra remove desire from the mind?

Sri Chinmoy: It depends on the individual seeker. If he has established abundant purity in his entire being, then it is only a matter of months. But if the seeker is not pure enough, then the mantra will take a very long time to produce the desired effect.

What is the purest Light?

Sri Chinmoy: The purest, highest Light is the Light of the Absolute Supreme. This Light can be seen and, at the same time, it can be felt or experienced. When we have established our constant, eternal and inseparable oneness with the Highest, the experience that we get is purest Light. If we have to define the purest Light, we can say that it is nothing but an experience of the Supreme in the Supreme. When we consciously feel our permanent and complete oneness with the Absolute Supreme, we get an eternal and everlasting experience of real, purest Light, and the purest consciousness of the Supreme is put at our disposal.

How can we attain the experience of purest Light?

Sri Chinmoy: We achieve this experience on the strength of our inner cry. If we work outwardly for material wealth or power, eventually we achieve these outer things. When we want to do something or achieve something, we have to work for it. Right now our goal is purest Light. In this case, our work is to cry inwardly. We have to inwardly cry like a child for inseparable oneness with the Supreme. The child cries for what it wants, and the mother always comes. No matter where she is, she comes to offer the child whatever it wants. Similarly, when we cry in the inmost recesses of our heart, our request is granted. But everything depends on the sincerity of our inner cry. If our cry is sincere, God is bound to grant it. If we cry inwardly for spiritual things – for Peace, Light, Bliss – then we are bound to achieve these divine qualities.

When you say, "Peace, Light and Bliss," what do you mean by Light? I keep trying to get a definition of Light and nobody is able to tell me.

Sri Chinmoy: Light is the power of the Supreme that illumines and transforms ignorance. Light is the capacity of the Supreme that transforms darkness into illumination-light. Anything that transforms our existence is Light. Light, you can say, is the life-breath of the Supreme.

Each colour of light has a special meaning. Blue Light is Infinity, vastness; white Light is purity. Green Light is freshness, life-energy, new life. Like that, each colour has a significance.

Guru, I often see Light as energy or forcefulness. Would you comment on that, please?

Sri Chinmoy: When you see Light as energy, you are absolutely correct. Light has tremendous energising power. When Light is not actively operating, it is the silent truth, the silent Brahman. But when Light operates in the form of energy, as you say, then it is the dynamic truth, the dynamic Brahman.

When you meditate, Light is operating in and through you. The Light which you get during your meditation is not only for your use but for others' use as well. When you receive Light, if you feel that you can use it at your sweet will, this is the wrong attitude. God gives us Light and He uses this Light in and through us for others. It is true that sometimes we misuse Light. We misuse Light when we want to possess the world for our own sake. But if we want to accept the world for God's sake, then we will never misuse Light. If we really want to accept the world for God's use, then at that time we don't try to possess the world. Consciously we jump into the sea of silence and activity. God gives us the opportunity or God Himself acts as the opportunity in the form of Light so that we can enter into the wide world. At that time, we do not possess anything; we just exercise our feeling of oneness.

If you want to help humanity – or rather, serve the Supreme in humanity – then from now on please try to have the feeling of oneness. Oneness will make you feel that there is only one reality and that is the soul. Only the feeling of oneness can cure the ills of humanity. Unless you have the feeling of oneness, you can never use Light properly and God can never use His Light in and through you.

Oftentimes I have the feeling or sensation that I see Light, but my mind doubts it very forcefully. I was wondering if the Light I see is real or imaginary.

Sri Chinmoy: If it is real Light, if it is pure, divine Light, then rest assured that your mind cannot doubt what you are seeing. The mind does not have the capacity to doubt divine Light while you are seeing it. If you are doubting it while seeing it, that means it is not the real Light that you are seeing. The effulgence of Light is such that it will not allow any mental suspicion or doubt to enter in. You cannot doubt while seeing Light if it is absolutely the purest Light of the divine Consciousness. When the real Light, divine Light, supreme Light appears, at that time the mind is obliterated; it does not function at all. The mind cannot exist when the divine Light comes. The entire being becomes all soul, all heart, all oneness.

The mind *does* have the capacity to doubt divine Light afterwards. First you see the Light and at that time the mind is divine. Then, after twelve hours or even five minutes, the mind will gather strength and try to throw suspicion into your experience of Light. When your consciousness descends, when the Light goes away from your physical awareness, at that time you can doubt the Light that you saw. If right now God stands before you, you are not going to doubt Him. But the moment God disappears from your outer vision, you can doubt God.

Because of your oneness with your body, you don't doubt your eyes, you don't doubt your nose. You know that you are part and parcel of your body and that your body is part and parcel of your life; so you don't doubt. Similarly, divine Light is your real existence. How can you deny or doubt your own existence? But after the experience is over, when you do not feel the Light as your own, at that time the mind may throw suspicion and doubt into you.

Can the physical consciousness lag behind, whereas the psychic consciousness is receiving higher light?

Sri Chinmoy: It has happened many, many times, thousands of times. The psychic consciousness is receiving Peace, Light and Bliss from above in abundant measure, whereas the physical consciousness is not powerful enough or large enough to hold it. So, what happens? Eventually the physical revolts and we suffer. That is why I tell the disciples, "Don't push, don't pull." Spirituality is a matter of accepting and transforming. We accept our life as it is; then we try to transform it. But we do not do it by hook or by crook. The divine means is through aspiration.

If we pull beyond our capacity, we will break. If a child wants to carry something very heavy, beyond his capacity, he will suffer. Slow and steady wins the race. Here capacity is receptivity. If we develop great receptivity, then no matter how high our spiritual height or how much we bring down from above, we will be able to assimilate it. If the container is very large, we don't have to worry. So when we aspire to climb up to the highest height, we have to aspire for expansion. Not only beginners, but also highly developed seekers have suffered from deplorable experiences. The physical revolts when it is not large enough to hold the Peace, Light and Power that the psychic brings down. So there should be a perfect harmony between the physical capacity and the heart's capacity.

III – Talks

Aspiration and God's Hour

When you speak of God's Hour, you have to know that it is the divine moment when God wants you to realise Him and to manifest Him here on earth. How can you harmonise God's Hour and your own aspiration? You will do your part. That is to say, you will play your own role most soulfully. You will meditate most soulfully. Every day before your meditation, you have to aim at a particular goal, and this particular goal is the highest Height, the transcendental Height that you are trying to reach. You can call it the Golden Shore of the Beyond. When the meditation is over, still you have not reached the Highest. Your intention or your soulful will was to reach the Highest, but still you have not reached it. If you feel sorry, if you feel miserable, then I wish to say that you will never be able to reach your goal.

Feel that there is a specific hour, a golden hour, when you are meant to reach your goal. God's Hour is not at your disposal; it belongs to God. At His sweet Will He will offer it to you, but you have every right to imagine that it is here in today's meditation. When today's meditation is over and God's Hour has not struck, do not feel miserable. Tomorrow again during your meditation you have every right to hope for God's Hour.

God's Hour is like a lotus. It blossoms petal by petal. There is a lotus deep within you, but it blooms only one petal at a time. When all the petals have bloomed, then it is a fully blossomed lotus. Like that, God's Hour is in our aspiration. You cannot separate God's Hour from your own aspiration. When your aspiration reaches the Highest, the acme of Perfection, then automatically the lotus which we call God's Hour blossoms fully.

My only request to you is not to try to push or pull. God has asked you to aspire, so you aspire.

Then it is up to God to give you divine victory. It is up to Him to fulfil your aspiration. Every day make your resolution: "This is what I am going to achieve." You are not trying to aggrandise or feed your ego. But you have to feel that if you can achieve your goal, if you can reach your destination, then only you will become a conscious instrument of the Supreme. Now, we are all instruments of the Supreme; all human beings are instruments of the Supreme. But most of us are unconscious instruments. We do not know that we are instruments; we think that we are the doer. But when we enter into the spiritual life, we come to feel that we are not the doer; somebody else is the doer and that somebody else is the Inner Pilot, the Supreme. Right now, just because you have your own individuality and personality, you have every right to feel that you are praying and you are meditating. Then a day will come when you will feel that it is not you who are praying and meditating; it is somebody else and that is the Supreme in you.

Everything depends on the goals you set. Today you may want God-realisation, but again tomorrow you may feel miserable, thinking that if you realise God, then you will not be able to enjoy the world. Early in the morning you may cry for Light, Peace and Bliss in infinite measure. You tell God that you can't exist without Him. But in the afternoon you may become a total stranger to your own aspiration. You may feel that if you realise God, then God will not allow you to enjoy teeming imperfections, vital life and all that. At that time, do you really want God or do you want the emotional life? Early in the morning God's Hour is fast approaching you but in the evening God's Hour becomes a far cry. The human difficulty is that in the morning you want something and in a few hours' time you want something else. So how can God's Hour call you? At every moment, aspire, aspire. In your aspiration, God's Hour is bound to strike.

Meditation and sincerity

Concentration, meditation and contemplation entirely depend on our inner cry. When a child is hungry, really hungry, he cries. He may be on the first floor and his mother on the third floor, but when the mother hears his cry she comes down immediately to feed the child.

Let us take concentration as an inner hunger. If we are really hungry, then our Father Supreme will come running no matter where we are crying. If we have intensity and sincerity in our cry, then I tell you that we can learn concentration in a few days' time. Otherwise, it can take years and years. And then, when will we have time to learn meditation and contemplation, which are more advanced subjects? There are people who have spent forty years learning how to concentrate. They have not developed an inner cry. It is like a good student and a bad student. A bad student will fail and fail and fail, whereas a good student will every year go on to a higher class.

Again, God-realisation is not like drinking water; it is not like instant coffee, something that you will get immediately. No, it takes time. If somebody says that he will be able to make you realise God overnight, then do not take him seriously. You have been to school, to college and university. It has taken you twenty years to get your Master's degree, which is based on outer knowledge. God-realisation, which is infinitely more important and more significant, naturally will take many more years. In no way do I want to discourage you. Only I wish to say that if your hunger is sincere and if you are desperately in need of God, then if you need the power of concentration, I assure you that God will give you the power of concentration.

There is also something practical you can do to strengthen your concentration-power. Please feel that inside your mind there is a room and naturally there is also a door. Stand either inside the room or outside the room, just in front of the door, and wait there to see who is coming. As soon as you see that some people are coming – "people" here means thoughts – you just keep the door closed. In the beginning, in order to become strong, you do not allow anybody in. Otherwise, while you are allowing friends to come in, your enemies may also come in and then you will be totally lost. But there comes a time when you become inwardly strong and you are in a position only to let your friends come in. At that time you will allow your friends in and let the enemies remain outside.

Good thoughts are your friends. Thoughts about self-sacrifice and loving God are good thoughts. So when these good thoughts want to enter into your room, you just leave the door open. But as soon as you see bad thoughts like fear, doubt, jealousy, frustration, depression and so on, you will keep the door closed.

If we practise concentration and meditation regularly, then we are bound to succeed. If we are really sincere, then we will reach the goal. But our difficulty is that we are sincere for one day or for one week and then we feel that spirituality is not meant for us. We want to realise God overnight. If we can't get our God-realisation overnight, then we think, "All right, let me pray for one week, one month, one year. After one year, if I don't realise God, I will give up." We feel that the spiritual life is not meant for us; it is only for others. It is like turning on the stove. If you turn the handle just a little and then stop, there will be no flame. You have to turn the handle to a certain spot and only then the flame will appear. But you move the handle only a little and then you think, "There will be no flame, so the best thing is to bring the handle back or to leave it where it is." This is what happens. People go one step and then they feel that God is not there. But God is standing at the end of two steps. If we don't go to where He is, then how are we going to see Him?

IV – Hartford television interview

First interviewer: I've heard about meditation, but I really don't know too much about it. This morning our guest is Sri Chinmoy, who is an expert in the area of meditation. He has lectured at many universities and written several books on the subject, and he also conducts twice-weekly meditations at the United Nations. It's nice to have you here this morning, Sri Chinmoy.

Sri Chinmoy: I am so happy to be here.

First interviewer: I think my first question is that I want to know more about meditation. Is it a mental exercise or is it like self-hypnosis? Is it an alternative to religion? Do people meditate instead of going to church?

Sri Chinmoy: Meditation is not a mental exercise, it is not self-hypnosis and it is not a form of religion. Meditation is an inner study for self-discovery. We meditate in order to empty our mind and in order to empty our heart. When we empty our mind we receive God the Peace. When we empty our heart we receive God the Love. Peace and Love are the two most important things in our life.

First interviewer: I think a lot of people are going to be wondering how you go about meditating. How do you do it? I think the results you are talking about sound good, but most of us don't really know how to meditate.

Sri Chinmoy: I wish to meditate for a few seconds. Then I shall explain how to meditate. [Sri Chinmoy meditates for a moment.] You just observed as I meditated for a couple of seconds. While I was meditating, I felt Peace and Delight all through my body. It was like a stream of Peace, Light and Delight flowing from the crown of my head to the soles of my feet.

Second interviewer: How would you describe what you saw in your mind's eye? Were you seeing some sort of a landscape scene?

Sri Chinmoy: Actually I was not seeing anything. I was growing into something, and that something was flowing Peace, Light and Bliss. I was becoming part and parcel of it.

First interviewer: Do you have to actually clear your mind of everything?

Sri Chinmoy: Yes, you have to clear your mind and not allow any thought whatsoever to enter into the mind. If a thought does enter into the mind, then we cannot grow into the divine Reality.

First interviewer: But I think that's really hard for people, because particularly in everyday life, there are so many things that are acting upon you. How do you go about actually clearing the mind and not thinking about something you have to do that day or a problem you have?

Sri Chinmoy: Meditation should be a regular practice. We study regularly in order to pass our examination or achieve something. If we practise daily, it is quite possible to meditate well. But to start with, we should read a few spiritual books to inspire ourselves and go to a spiritual Master who can increase our aspiration. We should try to live a regular, self-disciplined life.

First interviewer: So one can actually go to a class to learn?
Sri Chinmoy: Yes.

Second interviewer: What are some of the exercises? What can you learn from reading a book about how to empty your mind and heart? How would the readings inspire you to be able to do this?

Sri Chinmoy: If you read a spiritual book, it will mention techniques for emptying your mind and illumining your mind. But as regards physical exercises, I feel they are not absolutely necessary. These preliminary exercises help us to a certain extent, but they are not indispensable. When we sit and make our mind calm, quiet and tranquil, we feel that we are in a position to have a free access to our inner reality. When we have a free access to our inner reality, we hear the Message of God. God is constantly speaking to us. He is trying to guide us all the time, but it is we who do not hear His Message.

Second interviewer: When we are getting ready to meditate, doesn't the environment have to be just right? Do you have to be in a quiet place alone or can you do it with a bunch of people around?

Sri Chinmoy: It depends on your capacity. In the beginning it is impossible to meditate when there are people around who are making noise or who are not aspiring. But there comes a time when you become an expert in meditation. Then, no matter what is happening around you, you will not be affected at all.

Second interviewer: We are talking with the distinguished authority on Yoga and meditation, Sri Chinmoy. Sir, what about the housewife who is at home with three screaming children in the morning or most of the day? Or the business executive who is just running from here to there for appointments all day long? How can they sit down and take a few moments to meditate? How can you get them to calm down from their daily activities?

Sri Chinmoy: Housewives and business executives can easily meditate, provided they know what is most important in life and provided they are willing to do the first thing first. Early in the morning before they enter into the hustle and bustle of life, if they offer a few seconds to God, then they can easily meditate. God is for everyone. He is not the sole monopoly of one individual who is ready to aspire all the time. Just because God is omnipresent, He is in everybody. God is not denied to a housewife or a business executive; only they have to feel a conscious necessity for God.

Second interviewer: In the midst of daily life, how is a housewife going to sit down and take time out? Is there some simple thing she can do to relieve the tension?

Sri Chinmoy: Yes, while she is talking to her children, while she is trying to discipline their life, if she can feel the presence of the living God inside them, then there will be a spontaneous flow of divine love from her. And at that time her children will feel that their mother has something special to offer. So when she consciously observes God or feels the presence of God, she will be in a position to deal with her children in a divine way; and that is her meditation.

First interviewer: I've read about classes that you can go to and some seem very expensive, something like 300 dollars for a class. Do you feel there is commercialism in meditation?

Sri Chinmoy: It depends on the individual teacher. I have no idea what others do. In my case, I always say that my fee is aspiration or an inner cry, plus regularity.

I have been teaching meditation for the last seven or eight years, and we have about forty-five meditation Centres all over the world. If one has an inner cry and at the same time is willing to come to the Centre regularly and devotedly, then he has paid his fees.

Second interviewer: You mentioned the presence of God a number of times, and that would lead to another question: Is this God compatible with every religion that anybody might belong to?

Sri Chinmoy: Yes, every religion speaks about God. Yoga is another name for spirituality. Meditation also talks about God.

First interviewer: *I remember reading in the paper one day about certain scientific studies in terms of the physical effects that meditation has on the body. What are some of these?*

Sri Chinmoy: If we meditate well, then we feel peace inside ourselves. We feel that all the time there is illumining guidance within ourselves or a beckoning hand which is all the time leading us towards our destination, which is satisfaction-life.

First interviewer: So meditation can also decrease blood pressure and do other things?

Sri Chinmoy: These things can be done by the Will of God. When we meditate, we identify ourselves consciously with God's adamantine Will. So if we are in need of something, then naturally our God, who is all Love and all Compassion, will do the needful within us.

Second interviewer: Peace and love are wonderful things to have and we should all have them. But what do you do if you are trying to express a feeling of peace and love but people around you are running here and there, backstabbing and what-not in the everyday business world, let us say? How can this really help the situation?

Sri Chinmoy: In this world we feel that everything is contagious. If we can increase the number of people who are in the world of love and peace, then naturally we will be able to inspire and influence others. You are a good soul. If you work with a bad human being, then your inner good qualities will try to inspire that person. When we see a saint, immediately we feel the good qualities of the saint coming forward in ourselves and inspiring us. So if you have peace and love, then either today or tomorrow your peace and love will spread, because the very nature of peace is to spread and the very nature of love is to spread.

Second interviewer: I think, though, that a lot of people will look upon somebody who is meditating and so on as kind of weird, bizarre or mystical. How do you counter that feeling?

Sri Chinmoy: Right now let them cherish this false notion. But a day will come when we are in a position to offer or reveal our inner qualities and then they will be able to recognise their folly. So let them assess us in their own way. Let us offer to the world at large what we have to offer. A day will come when they will be able to recognise their mistake.

First interviewer: Thank you very much for coming today, Sri Chinmoy. I think people will now want to at least try meditation and see if it works for themselves.

Notes

p.131: On 8 May 1974, Sri Chinmoy was interviewed on a Hartford, Connecticut television show. This is a transcript of the interview.

Appendix

Bibliography

Sri Chinmoy:
 –*Aspiration-flames*, New York, Agni Press, 1974.
 –*Aspiration and God's Hour*, New York, Agni Press, 1977.

Table of contents

Aspiration-Flames
Aspiration-Flames   3

Aspiration and God's Hour
I – Meditation   75
II – Light   111
III – Talks   123
IV – Hartford television interview   131

Appendix
Bibliography   145

Table of contents

*Composition typographique par imprimerie
Ab Academia Aoidon, Paris & Lyon.*

*Un grand merci à Prof Knuth pour
l'utilisation avancée de TeX.*

A LYON, LE 7 JUIN LXXXIX Æ.G.

The heart-traveller

1. Aspiration-Flames – Aspiration and God's Hour
2. A Sri Chinmoy primer
3. Everest-Aspiration
4. New Year's Messages from Sri Chinmoy (1966–2007)

www.ingramcontent.com/pod-product-compliance
Lightning Source LLC
Chambersburg PA
CBHW031116080526
44587CB00011B/989